THE AMAZING CAREER OF
THE MARQUIS DE SADE

A STUDY OF THE CHARACTER AND VIEWS OF THE MAN
WHOSE FANTASTIC WORKS GAVE RISE TO
THE WORD SADISM

By JOSEPH McCABE

FOREWORD

The character of few men of modern times has been so fiercely disputed as that of the Marquis de Sade, the French writer whose fantastic works gave rise to the word sadism. Geoffrey Gorer prefixes to his "Revolutionary Ideas of the Marquis de Sade," the best study of what is called his philosophy, the estimates of him of a large number of writers. Nearly half of them describe his as "that atrocious and bloody blasphemer" "this frantic and abandoned collector of all the crimes and all the filth," "this frenzied pornographer," "this strange abortion," etc.

To others he is "one of the glories of France" or "one of the greatest of writers," while so severe and distinguished a critic as Sainte-Beuve thinks him "one of the great inspirers of us moderns," and Professor J. B. S. Haldane who writes a preface to Gorer's far from depreciatory work, leniently says that he was "a remarkable man who was the victim both of himself and of his fellow-men," and that in some aspects of social idealism "he went far beyond even the most advanced social thinkers of our day."

Even phrenologists (who found his bumps quite normal) graphologists and psychologists—what novelties we shall read when our psychiatrists hear of him—have tried their arts on the enigma of his character, but it remains poised between—I would not say between heaven and hell—but at least between earth and hell.

The account of his career is sometimes "A Story of Bluebeard for Adults," sometimes the common story of a pervert, sometimes the record of a misunderstood and persecuted pioneer of a greater age than ours. So this little work, it is hardly necessary to say, makes no pretence of having solved the enigma. But I have made a fresh study of the documents and a careful comparison of the divergent accounts of his career, some of which frankly use the imagination to embroider the facts, some deny or ignore uncongenial facts, and some assume that the reader welcomes picturesque or spicy gossip even more eagerly than facts.

With this plain statement of established facts and sober probabilities and with a larger attention than is usually given to the historical background I offer the reader the material for testing my estimate of the growth and final stage of this strange personality.

1: IN THE GAYEST DAYS OF PARIS

Louis Donatian Alphonse Francois, Marquis de Sade, was born in Paris on June 2nd, 1740. The age is significant but the great world about him has no meaning for a puling infant and we will consider it presently. His heritage throws no light on his character; as, in spite of the modern stress on it, it rarely does. The father of this prodigy of mental turbulence, this man of "the wildest imagination that ever terrified mankind," was a cold calculating diplomat, the correct and haughty representative of one of the oldest and most distinguished noble families of Provence. The mother, a niece of the great Cardinal Richelieu, a lady of high aristocratic connections, seems to have been a fitting partner for such a man; and as neither of them lived long enough to see the ugliness of their duckling, we dismiss them from the story.

The boy Alphonse was born in one of the largest palaces of the nobility in Paris, that of the Prince de Conde, perhaps the greatest of the nobles. His mother was distantly related to the Princess and became her leading *dame d' honneur* or companion. But the formidable, frowning palace, with spacious Italian garden—it sold later in the century for $8,000,000—was not one of those Parisian mansions in which the windows blazed and the gold clinked on the gambling tables until dawn. Indeed the head of the house was in exile in the provinces, trying to forget in a deep study of science the political career that had ended in disaster.

Alphonse was, in any case, not there long enough to receive deep impressions. He says somewhere that he, then a child with blue eyes and blond curls and a quick temper, played with the Princess's son in the noble gardens, until one day he fell in fury on the boy and had to be taken away. Louis Joseph was, in fact, four years older than Alphonse . . . But, the truth is that the Count de Sade and his wife were sent to the embassy at Cologne and the Princess went to live in the country, so Alphonse, at the age of 3 or 4, was taken on the long coach ride to his grandmother's house at Avignon.

Neither does his education throw any light on his later development. His grandmother spoiled the pretty boy as grandmothers do, but when he was old enough to approach the three R's he was sent to a village in Auvergne, where an uncle of his was the priest, and he remained there until he was 10. There seems to be sufficient evidence that the aristocratic priest had really repented of his earlier gaities—he was then absorbed in writing his 3-volume life of Petrarch—and we must not imagine Alphonse prematurely learning the facts of life from one of the numerous light-living abbes of the time. However, at the age of 10, he was brought back to Paris and entered at the famous Jesuit College of Louis le Grand.

Forty years earlier it had had a brilliant pupil named Francois Arouet, who was now known to all France as Voltaire, the ablest writer and most daring rebel in the country. Alphonse was neither brilliant nor diligent, and it is the development of his character that interests us. Years later, the Jesuits pointed out that in their archives there was a note that said that the day he left was "a festival for the college." "The youth," it said, "already had a detestable air that made him odious to everybody. He was already a fanatic of vice." That was obviously written decades later. But the Jesuit fathers were too

5

wise to impose severe restraints on the sons of the noble and wealthy on whose education they specialized, and as Alphonse reached sexual maturity in that period and we know the weaknesses of such colleges, we wonder. Except that the Jesuits had themselves a repute for sodomy, we have no details, and in any case it was the state of Paris and France, of which he was now becoming sensible, that would make the deeper impression on him.

British and American writers on him do not sufficiently appreciate the background of his early career, and their readers are apt to imagine him as a moral portent appearing in an age that was comparable to ours. Catholic readers, particularly, are led to think that France, being still overwhelmingly loyal to the faith, was also normally virtuous until Voltaire and Rousseau, Diderot and Helvetius, undermined its morals with their skepticism.

It is one of the fairy-tales with which we have replaced the fables of the Middle Ages. It is a platitude of French history that the country had just had a period of extraordinary license, while Voltaire and Rousseau were still boys and there was not an Atheist on the horizon. Louis XIV, the Monarch of Many Mistresses, had been penitent and pious in the last 20 years of his life. He had also been impotent. At his death in 1715 he had left only a great-grandson of the age of 5, and the Duke of Orleans had taken over the Regency. There were eight years of unprecedented license. As Cardinal Dubois shared the orgies in the royal palace, the whole higher clergy were infected. The distinguished French historian Martin, who was not noticeably anti-clerical, says of this period in his classic "History of France";

"There was never anything in history to equal the group of cardinals round Dubois, supported by a large number of archbishops and bishops. It was a Conclave of Satan in which simony, dishonesty, incest, and sodomy were crowned with the Red Hat. The French Church no longer existed except in fragments of the wreck floating in the flood."

The nobles, and the common clergy and laity, were not insensible of the example. In the period from the accession of Louis XV (1723) to the Revolution, Martin says, "sensuality was worse than ever," but it was more polished. Manners were exquisite, and a spirit of cold calculation, in matters both of love and politics, pervaded the higher classes. The church leaders—Cardinal de Rohan (of the Diamond Necklace romance), Archbishop de Brienne (proposed for the see of Paris, but the King said: "Surely the Archbishop of Paris ought to be a man who believes in God"), Archbishop Dillon, etc., no more concealed their amours than the King did. Society took its cue, and all the gossip of Paris would pass through aristocratic homes to aristocratic colleges like Louis le Grand, reaching the ears of the idle and precociously stimulated Alphonse de Sade.

He would see a little of court-life himself when, at the age of 14, his father got him admitted to the select corps of the Light Horse, the King's special bodyguard, with gold-embroidered banners of white taffeta and the most gorgeous uniforms in the French Army. There were only 20 officers and 200 men—or boys and youths—and the official geneologist had to go deep into de Sade's lineage before he was accepted. They were stationed at Versailles, which hummed with gossip and intrigue. At the age of 16 he was transferred to the carabineers, another royal regiment, with the standard of a golden sun on a ground of blue silk.

In that year Damiens attempted the life of the king, and doubtless Alphonse would go with all Paris to see the torture and execution of the man in the great square. The flesh was torn from his bones with red-hot hooks, boiling lime was poured on his wounds, and four horses, pulling in different directions tore his body asunder. Even in 1767 you did not need much imagination to picture horrors. It

6

is another element of de Sade's background that is too often forgotten.

The Seven Years War against Prussia and England broke out and he became a captain of cavalry. We know nothing reliable about his experiences in Germany and can easily accept his word that he fought "with that frenzy that men call bravery." Toward the end of the war his regiment was cut up, and with the survivors he was sent into barracks in a dull small town of Normandy.

He was now 22 years old, a young man of established character, if we may so describe the kind of character that such an education in such an age would form. In the more serious meaning of the word he showed no character at all. He was a cork floating on the surface of the frothy stream of the life of his caste.

Some writers hold that he was a pioneer of Nietzsche and Stirner in philosophic individualism. How he developed later we shall see, but at this stage, and for years afterwards, he did not attack rules and conventions, which had not yet put the least restraint on his impulses. He hardly knew that they existed. He just plucked whatever fruit he found ripe. Every young officer had a mistress, so he had one. She was the sister of a brother-officer.

The war ended in a few months and he was recalled to Paris. His father had returned from Cologne and felt that it was time to see his son married. Holy matrimony was in France in those pious days a business arrangement with as little romance as the mating of prize cattle. The parents sought among their acquaintances for a "suitable" mate for their sons, the chief qualifications being a reasonable promise of fertility and a good dowry. If they had none they tried one of the professional agents. But the Count de Sade was a friend of one of the chief judges of Paris, President de Montreuil, who had two daughters and could give them heavy dowries. The elder Renee-Pelagie, was 23: and for a wealthy girl with a determined and influential mother to remain so long unmarried suggests "a spot on the peach," as the French say. The biographers describe her as beautiful—in biography, as in fiction, the bride is nearly always beautiful—sedate, and virtuous.

If the portrait of her in Desbordes is genuine she was not beautiful, but had a broad puffy face and figure that would not appeal to a dashing cavalry captain and epicure. Her character is obscure. She clung to her husband in spite of his wild and scandalous life and two terms in prison, until he had completely dissipated her dowry on other women and was generally discredited. It seems to me that she was a woman of colorless personality, who just clung to him as long as she could for the sake of her home and family and then listened to her imperious mother and left him.

Some biographers offer us a neat little romance at this stage. The marriage is arranged, not in heaven but in Mme de Montreuil's boudoir, and Alphonse is taken to see Renee. She strikes no spark, but he sees her young sister Louise, a charming and vivacious girl of 16, fresh from the convent, and falls in love with her. But mamma is adamant. He must marry the elder and he has to yield. This, says Almeras, was the cause of his perverse practices. The truth is that the two families were so well acquainted that he had often seen both girls. I would not say that he decided to accept Renee's dowry, with a priestly blessing thrown in, but secure an illicit connection with the younger girl. He had to marry Renee, and it was years before Louise yielded to his spirited and protracted siege. But a few weeks after the superb ceremony in the most fashionable church of Paris, the noble connections of the two parties and the captain's aristocratic officer-friends making a brave show—one writer says that the King and Queen were present—Alphonse. in the elegant language of Holy Writ, returned to his vomit.

There was, of course, a minority

of really strict Catholics in every age, but the great majority, seeing the complacency with which the Jesuit confessors regarded the open amours of Louis XIV and Louis XV, considered it quixotic to expect a young husband to confine his embraces to his wife. At that time the monotony was largely relieved by making mistresses of each other's wives, but the men had, besides the usual solace, "little houses," as the French called them, or love-nests in which they kept a mistress or indulged in an occasional orgy. It seems that the Marquis had set up one of these love-nests as soon as he returned to Paris. It was a small house, modestly named "The Almonry," at Arcueil, an old village then about three miles south of Paris, a short run on horse or in a carriage. It was now re-opened and doubtless redecorated out of the dowry; for Alphonse had himself only an income of a few thousand a year from a lieutenant-governorship in the provinces which his father had passed on to him. These little houses often had an Arabian Nights atmosphere. They shone with silks and brocades and were adorned with costly pieces of erotic sculpture and printing.

The Almonry was soon one of the best known of the little houses, for Alphonse had joined one of the fastest and most elegant sets—the Duc de Fromsac, the Prince de Lamballe, etc.—in Paris. To Arcueil they brought actresses, selected ballet-girls, and the choicer courtesans that the owners of the "big houses" hired out occasionally.

Two expensive actresses were de Sade's chief playmates, but he seems from the first frequently to have hired common girls for a rougher type of entertainment. The rumor of orgies spread in the village and reached Paris. There were stories of aphrodisiacs, of actresses dressed as nuns, of obscene novelties.

In October the police arrested de Sade and lodged him in the grim fortress-jail of Vincennes. It was the beginning of what we may call the specific education of the Mar-

quis. From his elegant apartment in Paris and his nest at Arcueil, he passed to a damp dark cell with small, barred windows, a primitive bed, and rough food.

His letters betray his extreme nervousness and chargin. He even professes repentance for his sins, and asks for a priest! He gets his wife and her mother to use all the influence they can to obtain his release, but for weeks the officials reply that the King regards his offence as serious and he must remain in jail.

What the offence was we do not know. As Louis XV was in a few years to surrender to the glorified whore Madame Du Barry, daughter of a seamstress, one wonders what it was that provoked his moral indignation. Desbordes points out that in his work "The 120 Days of Sodom," de Sade speaks of a young duke who began at the age of 23 to "find pleasure in the sufferings of others" and suggests that he had been detected in the practice of what a later writer called sadism.

Generally biographers say, without authority, that he was involved in "a row in a brothel" which would hardly merit a month or two in Vincennes. Others point out that President de Montreuil had deadly rivals in the judiciary and the police, and they may have initiated that police vigilance which began at that time. We should remember, in any case, that until the Revolution it was hardly necessary to commit any crime at all to be sent to the Bastille or Vincennes. Remember the Man in the Iron Mask. A royal letter served instead of a trial and sentence. Broadly, I would conclude that a charge of some sort of perversity, which would horrify the normally adulterous King, was brought against the Marquis.

When he was released from Vincennes he was ordered to keep away from Paris for a time, and he went with his wife to live in the strict atmosphere of her mother's country chateau. Here he could not get even the consolation of seducing Louise, who was sent back to a convent in Paris. He was allowed to return in 1764 but we have a note of the chief of police warning the owner or manager of one of the "big houses" that he must not hire out girls to the Marquis de Sade. It appears that he now attached Mlle. de Beauvoisin, a robust (if not vulgar), expensive, and notorious gold-digger whose lack of beauty in face or figure must have had some other compensation. He took her to an isolated estate near Abt, a few score miles from Marseilles, which belonged to his family.

In the old and long almost deserted castle of La Coste he took his revenge for what he considered the affront to his nobility. These folk at Paris, without even the grace to be hypocritical—the wildest stories circulated about the King and some of the highest nobles and ecclesiastics—had put the descendant of several centuries of counts in a foul and infamous dungeon on some complaint of a common prostitute.

He began to harden in his moral defiance. We have letters from and to his priest-uncle and a nun-aunt from which we gather that he lit up the simple countryside. They even charge him with passing off Mlle. de Beauvoisin, with whom no lady would have remained in the same room, as his wife. But we have no more than a general idea of dissipation and debauch with actresses, professionals, and servants, until he reappears in Paris in 1767. He had not yet lost caste. His first child was baptized with high ceremony in the most fashionable church of Paris. The godfather was the Prince de Condé: the godmother the Princess Conti.

We have a letter, dated a few months after the baptism, in which the chief of the Paris police remarks that there is a good deal of talk about "the horrors of M. le Conte de Sade." He obviously means the Marquis, who did not take the title of Count even when his father died in 1774. The official says that a story is going round that the Marquis has failed to attract a popular actress of the Opera with an offer of 25 louis (about $250) a month to spend her leisure with him at Arcueil. His wife's dowry was clearly melting away and he was forced to economize. And this presently led to a more serious scandal: to the virtual close of this part of his career as one of the bloods of the gay city and the opening of that phase which was to win him a dark immortality.

2. DE SADE BECOMES A SADIST

At 9 in the morning of Easter Sunday (April 3), 1768, the Marquis, elegantly dressed as usual, was crossing one of the squares in the city when a young woman accosted him for an alms. That, at least, was her testimony later. In broken French she explained that she was a native of Strassburg and had married a baker at Paris. He had deserted her and she was destitute.

De Sade told her that he wanted a housekeeper for his place at Arcueil: a proposal which even a nun in Paris could not have misunderstood. We need not take her word that she at first refused. She had clearly taken to the streets, and a rich and elegant patron would be a godsend.

He drove her to Arcueil, where, as was usual, a valet took care of his house and arranged for the cheaper visitors. Some hours later Rose Keller, as she was named, tumbled over the garden wall in tears and scanty attire, complaining to the few women who gathered round her that the monster in the Almonry had threatened her life and assaulted her in the most outrageous fashion. At the point of the pistol he had compelled her to strip and had tied her, face downward, on the bed. He had then beaten her on the appointed spot with a birch-rod and a stick until

9

she bled and with his pen-knife he had stabbed her in the same and even more delicate regions. He had poured molten wax on her wounds and locked her in the room.

When she had asked him to call a priest to hear her Easter confession before she died, the monster had said that he would hear it himself. However, she had broken her bonds, let herself down from the window by knotted sheets, and climbed over the garden wall. In those days a lady was quite willing to give ocular proof of her story in the public streets, so when the neighbors saw the stripes and the blood they hurried her to the police-station. They had long known that there was "something awful" going on in that house.

In substance, the woman's story was correct. Whipping hired women—the mildest and most common form of sadism—was not a novelty in France and is a practice described in all manuals of sexology. That he used a knife is most probably fiction or the frenzied woman's interpretation of cuts with the birch. It was a fortnight before she was examined by a competent doctor, and he found no wounds deeper than the skin. "There you are," said de Sade, gaily, to the police officials, "you ought to regard me as a public benefactor who has invented a salve that makes knife-wounds disappear in a few days." He admitted that he had put salve on the bruises. But he refused to take seriously a not uncommon brothel-incident like this, and it seems that the police were willing to overlook it for a few gold coins. But one of the near neighbors who had long been exasperated by the gaiety of the Almonry, an elderly judge and puritan, reported it to the Paris police, among whose leading officials there were men who detested the Marquis. There were also expert judicial officials who hated his father-in-law and would gladly discredit him.

The story ran through Paris and even reached London. The Marquise de Deffand, friend of Voltaire and one of the most brilliant women in France, sent an account of it to Horace Walpole, and it went through London clubs as well as those of Paris. Naturally, the story grew in interest. In the end it ran that de Sade and his friends had laid the lady nude on an operating table and begun to vivisect her, and that de Sade had a hole ready in his garden to receive the remains. One can imagine the horror of Mme. de Montreuil and her husband. She sent at once for a priest who had been the Marquis's tutor in his youth. He bribed Rosa, burned compromising letters and papers in the Marquis's apartment in Paris, and paid all his debts, while Mme. de Montreuil and the Marquise de Sade turned to their influential friends.

But, as I said, hostile officials were determined to force it to a trial. The police protested that the house at Arcueil, instead of being a quiet and decent house of sin as other little houses were, had long been notorious for orgies of both sexes.

Some French writers suggest that these pestiferous atheistic Encyclopedists had so disturbed the people —we are, remember, drawing nearer to the Revolution—that there were loud complaints of the immunity of the aristocrats with their orgies and gross extravagances, from the royal palace downward, while the country was reeling toward bankruptcy. The police, it is said, were directed to find a scapegoat.

It does at first sight seem singular that de Sade almost alone was selected for heavy punishment in so openly and generally corrupt a world. We cannot even suppose that the mild perversity he had as yet betrayed was uncommon. But, apart from the fact that he certainly had enemies in the police and his father-in-law had in the judiciary, probably those who did indulge abnormally were careful to conceal their actions.

Bishops and archbishops who took little trouble to hide their normal relations with the fine ladies of their circle shuddered to hear of a man stripping a woman of the street and laying the birch on her backside. However that may be, de Sade, who had been taken by his priest-tutor to the chateau of Saumur, was arrested there and imprisoned in the fortress of Pierre Ancine, the Bastille of Lyons. He was released in a few weeks and told to present himself in Paris for trial. Desbordes, who has the best collection of official documents in his "Vrai Visage Du Marquis de Sade" (1939), says that instead of obeying he went to the convent where Louise was enclosed—some say that she had been compelled to take the veil—and carried her off to La Coste.

It is difficult at many points to trace the real truth in the tangle of contradictions. The biography which Gorer prefixes to his able study of de Sade's ideas, on which the lengthy sketch in the Encyclopedia Sexualis is based, is uncritical and inadequate. If we follow Desbordes, de Sade's action raised the agitation against him to such a height that he was frightened. He came back to Lyons, where he had left his wife, and went with her to Paris.

But the imperious Mme. de Montreuil, who to this date fought his battles for him—or for her daughter—had won in the struggle of intrigues. The King had been induced to intervene. From the ordinary courts the case was removed by the King's order to the Grand Court and de Sade was taken under the royal protection. He and his valet were called on to make statements. Yes, he said, he had whipped the lady's backside with knotted cords; and he was ordered to pay 100 livres ($500) to the poor (probably to poor Rosa, who promptly married on it) and the case was dismissed.

But the chief of police warned him to keep out of Paris, and he went down to La Coste and again enlivened the quiet Provencal countryside. The house was a castle of the early medieval type that looks somber and massive in its ruins today. De Sade decorated it magnificently and built a theater in the grounds to which he brought companies from Marseilles, some 50 miles away.

For a time he was recalled to the army, but he was no longer popular. We can hardly suppose that the little scandal in Paris would do more than amuse brother-officers, and his character must have changed since the war-days; unless the boycott of him is a figment of his biographers, some of whom are fertile in such matters. When he returned to La Coste in 1771 and tried to resume his life of provincial splendor he soon ran into financial embarrassment.

I imagine that his new need to economize was largely responsible for what is called the second great scandal of his career, or the Case of the Poisoned Girls at Marseilles. In point of fact, it is, we shall see, the character of his writings that caused later writers to give his name to that particular form of sexual behavior. But for these works his name would have long since perished.

The first scandal had been in 1768: the second was in 1772. As I have said, the man who imagines that the life of France was then so orderly that these two not serious outrages committed by an army-officer on street-girls could cause a nation-wide sensation is ingenious. It was in 1769 that Louis XV presented the notorious courtesan Jeanne Du Barry, decorated with a coronet, for the homage of his courtiers. It was only a few years since a disreputable noble had picked her out of the gutters of Paris and she remained vulgar in the robes and jewels of a countess. The highest nobles and prelates bowed before her; at the very time when de Sade was sentenced to death for an unpleasant adventure in a brothel. Such things are part of the working of de Sade's mind.

About what actually occurred there is almost no dispute. In June, 1772, the Marquis went, with his valet, to Marseilles on business and decided to make it also an occasion of pleasure. For this he exchanged identities with his valet, which can hardly have deceived the girls, and it was the tall, lanky, pock-marked valet, in fine clothes and wearing a sword, with the disguised noble in the background, who visited the rooms of Marguerite Coste, in the old town in the morning of June 21.

De Sade had a gold and crystal box of candy or pastilles and gave her a few. They were of a type that was well known in France, Italy, and Spain in the 18th century, charged with cantharides (o r Spanish Fly). These flying beetles common in the South of France as well as Spain, are dried and ground and used for medical purposes. But in mild doses they are aphrodisiac and were then extensively used in candy for that purpose.

There is evidence that de Sade had been distributing them for some time to the girls and ladies who attended his balls and fetes at La Coste. In stronger doses the effect is morbid, and it would not be surprising if at this stage the Marquis made the dose strong to provide a spectacle. The girl became sick, and she was later induced to accuse him of poisoning her.

Through the valet La Tour, the Marquis had arranged a further entertainment. Three girls of the usual cheap type were engaged to meet him in a more respectable quarter. Desbordes gives us not only a photograph of the house but even one of the bedroom-door, as if they had become historic.

In short, De Sade admitted them one at a time and gave each a light whipping. He then produced a lash with nails or bent pins (more probably) in it and marks of dried blood on it—he had evidently used it at La Coste—and invited them to thrash him. Between wine and cantharides-pastilles they were all in a morbid state, but the instrument horrified the girls. He therefore sent one of them out for a birch-rod and with this the girls and the valet gave him 859 strokes.

The police later found the figures 215, 179, 225 and 240 scratched with a knife on the woodwork by de Sade. It seems to be the tally of each, with an interval. After this long spell of masochism we can imagine what happened.

Desbordes says that he dare not give the words of the police report at this point, but it is clear that it was something like one of the practices described by Victor Marguerite about 20 years ago as occurring in modern Paris in his novel "La Garconne." The police charge was sodomy and poisoning. The girls became hysterical and violently sick, and the sensation in the quarter reached the ears of the police. The report spread over France and is still sometimes repeated that two of them died, which is clearly false.

De Sade was certainly not insane at this time, but his excessive glandular activity, whipped up by the use of cantharides and now completely uncontrolled by a mind that was distorted by the spectacle of general hypocrisy, disposed him to experiment and find out every way in which he could find satisfaction. He knew nothing for a week after his return to La Coste of what was happening in Marseilles. The police had been called in and had soon learned his identity. The chemists failed to find any traces of arsenic which was at first alleged, and the other charge was one that the police did not usually press against a noble; or there would have been scandals in high places.

But the name of the Marquis de Sade caused the Marseilles police to communicate with the authorities in Paris, and they were presently directed to proceed rigorously. The police officials and judges —chiefly Maupeou, chief judge at Paris, a severe puritan,' a rival and enemy of de Sade's father-in-law, eagerly seized the charge and Mme. de Montreuil no longer proctected him. She had secured a chance of an engagement for Louise, and it suited her best that the Marquis should not be executed but detained for life in a fortress.

The provincial court therefore found de Sade and the valet guilty of sodomy and condemned them to death in their absence. They had fled as soon as de Sade learned that he was to be arrested. Most of the biographers here insert a fictitious romance. De Sade, they say, contacted Louise and persuaded her to fly with him to Italy, where she presently died; from, it is suggested, his brutality.

He is said to have wandered on to Rome where he was arrested in mistake as an absconding banker, then back to Savoy, where he was detected and arrested at Chambery. The ample documents given by Desbordes show that this is entirely false. Louise was at this time under the vigilant eye of her dragon of a mother, and, the father having ample means for a good dowry, they found a candidate for marriage in spite of her blotted record, but on condition that it— or de Sade—could be kept out of sight. It was Mme. de Montreuil who now pressed for the incarceration of the Marquis, outside France, for life. A dozen letters show this. In one of them Renee violently quarrels with her mother for prosecuting her husband.

From these documents the course of events is clear, and is as romantic as any novel. De Sade and his valet fled in disgust to Chambery which, being in Savoy, was then in the dominions of the King of Sardinia, not in France. The de Sade family, including the priest and the nun and the great uncles who were gay members of the Templar Order, met in council and made over all that was left of the property to Renee who, apparently, secretly provided her husband with funds. But Mme. de Montreuil's spies discovered him and, stipulating that he receive a sentence of life-imprisonment instead of death, she told the authorities at Paris.

They gave his address to the Sardinian ambassador, and he was arrested in December and put in the fortress of Miolan near the town. In this pleasant chateau, as it was, framed in the soft hilly scenery of Provence, the Marquis, who gave his word of honor that he would make no attempt to escape, was intended to spend the remainder of his life. He had considerable freedom and comfort, his valet and a servant, a bastard of

genial fellow prisoner in Baron d'Allee. They gambled heavily and in a letter to his authorities the the Duke of Bavaria, and a congovernor says that the servant shared in their "debauches." We understand.

But even with this characteristic consolation de Sade was infuriated, and he got his wife to storm Paris and the Sardinian court with representations that her mother was, for her own objects, keeping an innocent man from his home and family. When she made no progress, she entered on an astonishing adventure. I have observed from the start that the biographers' description of her as "beautiful, gentle, and virtuous" is open to question, but to this point she has been a shadowy and enigmatic figure in the background of mystery. She was entirely aware—we shall presently see clear proof of this—of her husband's practices and it may be thought that she remained with him and bore him three children out of meekness. She now made a plot, in the vein of the Three Musketeers, to rescue him and bring him to La Coste. She came to Chambery and hired and armed 15 tramps. She smuggled a letter to her husband in jail telling him of her arrangements, and on the night of April 30th, after distributing a few bribes, de Sade, his valet, the equally unscrupulous royal bastard and Baron d'Alee (a suspected murderer) climbed over the wall. The 15 amateur musketeers closed round them and, with Renee on horseback bringing up the rear they made by devious paths for the Swiss frontier. They pushed on to Italy but by December felt that they could return to La Coste.

The castle was, from years of neglect, as grim inside as it was without, but they all set to work to throw out the broken furniture, clean up the richly decorated rooms, and repair the drawbridge, which they could close against the police. The theater was closed and weeds were suffered to choke the approaches. Here the Marquis and Marquise, with their three children and three or four servants, settled down on a reduced income, to an uncertain life. But there was a villain in the romance.

De Sade's solicitor or steward, and (he believed) friend, was secretly in the pay of Mme. de Montreuil and he sent word at once to her. Within a fortnight a police agent and four archers (the name was still kept for the police) reached La Coste from Paris. It was easy for de Sade to hide while they searched the castle, and Renee wrote a furious letter to her mother.

The summer months passed quietly, if dully and penuriously and Renee went to Paris in the autumn and her mother, pretending to be reconciled, promised her that she was pressing for a revision of the death-sentence. Meantime the place was held ready for a siege. By day a watch was kept from a tower. At night the doors were bolted and no light shown. Parents, children and the few servants dragged out the winter on short rations. "How far this seems to be from libertinage," Desbordes reflects.

But de Sade was never "far from libertinage." The staff consisted of two young girls of 13 or 14, whom Renee had brought from Lyons to be trained as servants, two young women as chamber maid and cook, and a rustic boy of 15 whom de Sade called his secretary, though the boy—I have read one of his letters—could hardly spell a word of two syllables. His function was clear and Renee must have known it, as she must have more or less expected the fate of the girls.

Rumors began again to spread in the neighboring town of Apt and at last in Lyons. The parents of the younger girls complained to the police, and they insisted on entering the castle and examining the girls; on whom they said, they found bruises.

Before anything further could be done Renee sent one young girl to the home of de Sade's priest-uncle and the other to his nun-aunt. Then the chambermaid Nanon was found to be pregnant and she turned bitterly against de Sade.

She went to swell the charges at Lyons with complaints of seduction and flagellation. Renee's conduct here disposes us to take the darker view of her character instead of accepting the pictures of her as a tender and virtuous woman clinging to a sinful husband from sheer sense of duty.

She informed the police that the girl had stolen three silver dishes, which she (the Marquise) buried in the garden, and she asked her mother to get a *lettre de cachet* (royal order) to put the girl in prison without trial. It was done, and the girl had her baby in prison, where it died of neglect. At the same time the mother of the boy "secretary" turned up at Aix and added to the list of charges against the Marquis, although Renee took the boy to Aix and got him to deny the charges. Presently the girl who had been put in the care of the priest-uncle escaped and was taken to Lyons to confirm his charge.

De Sade, now alone, ill and alarmed by the cloud on every horizon, raised funds and fled to Italy. The documents show that it is here that we have to place his Italian journey. He was in Florence in August, 1775, in Naples in the Spring. Here he, having concealed his name, was mistaken by the police for an absconding French bank-clerk and arrested. But he escaped and with his valet he stealthily made his way to the frontier.

They crossed it by the goat-paths on the mountains (July, 1776) and returned to Province. It is amusing to read how, as he drew near La Coste, he saw notices posted up that there was to be a theatrical performance of the loose comedy *Le mari cocu* ("The Cuckold Husband"), and he indignantly forbade it. It was, he says in a letter, "scandalous and an affront to the Church." His lawyer explaining this new "devotion" of the Marquis says to a friend that in Italy he had had an audience of the Pope! We smile again when we read that several large trunks of baggage followed his arrival at La Coste. They were full of indelicate marbles and other "antiquities" that he had bought in Italy. Indeed he had not long been back when his cook's father called at the castle and accused him of . . . . Desbordes has to cut the next few words out of the text of the manuscript. We can supply them. The cook told her father that he was a liar, and, after a choicely worded wrangle, the Marquis threw him out. He turned on de Sade with a pistol, but it misfired. However, he came back with four robust friends and had another shot, which missed; while his daughter refused to quit her abode of love.

A few more weeks of this miserable life passed, and de Sade was then awakened one night to receive an anonymous warning from Paris that he was to be arrested. Desbordes thinks, plausibly enough, that the warning came from Louise, for it was her mother who had got the decree of arrest. Now seriously alarmed, de Sade went to consult his priest-uncle and was told that he must either go to Paris and submit or fly again. They started for Paris—preceded by a 10-page letter of invective from Renee to her mother—and arrived there on March 10th, 1777. De Sade learned that his mother had died in a convent a week earlier, and next morning he went to the cemetery. But the faithless steward had informed Mme. de Montreuil, who had warned the police, and they arrested him and lodged him in the fortress-prison of Vincennes.

3. BROODING IN THE SHADOWS

Everybody has heard of that grim feudal prison, the Bastille, which the people of Paris tore down in the first fervor of the Revolution. Few will know that a mile or two away, buried in the lovely forest of Vincennes beyond the walls was another prison at the disposal of the despotic monarch.

For centuries a fortified royal castle, it had been turned into a sort of annex of the Bastille and had held some illustrious prisoners in its formidable gate-tower. At the time when the Marquis de Sade was taken to it there were only two other prisoners in it, and the French Grande Encyclopedie observes that these, as well as de Sade, were regarded as unbalanced in mind.

Gorer inclines to the opinion that de Sade was really considered by the authorities to be a man of advanced political opinions. His experiences would not have encouraged him to regard the political system, with all its corruption, incompetence, and hypocrisy, with loyalty and admiration, but it seems to me that he had not as yet gone on from rebellious feelings to definite anti-monarchic opinions.

It was understood that he was to await in Vincennes the revision of the sentence of the Aix court, but month followed month without any news of progress toward a revision, and he was treated with a severity that would better have fitted a condemned murderer. He was confined to a dim, dank, stone cell with narrow, barred window, and rarely permitted any exercise.

The food, which was a torture to his palate, was thrust through a hole in the door. He was not allowed to have books or pen or ink, he could send and receive only one letter a week, and his wife was rarely permitted to visit him. Here, although everybody knew that the charge of poisoning on which he had been condemned to death was false, he had to spend the bitterest year of his life. His children wrote him affectionate letters occasionally—Papa was abroad, they were told—but his correspondence with his wife betrayed almost a tinge of insanity. When Renee assured him week by week that "it would not be long now" yet the summer months dragged on and he was tormented with rage and suspicion.

She was in league with her mother to keep him there, he said, or she had found a lover in Paris and did not want him released. The letters are pitiful. It is said that he put obscene remarks or drawings on the letters he received from her.

She tried the poor trick of writing a few lines in lemon juice but she had nothing more to say than what was written in ink and it was futile. One idea began to dominate his mind. It was acknowledged that he was innocent, yet the whole world conspired to destroy his sanity or his life.

He was still, we must remember, only 38 years old, and he must have been a man of robust physique. After years of unrestricted and artificially-stimulated sex-life, the solitary confinement must have been a torture, exacerbated by the sordid conditions in which he found himself after a life of luxury. And all this for, as he says in one letter, "smacking the bottom of a whore."

After a few months he fell into a habit which seemed to suggest that his mind was failing. He would count the number of words, syllables or letters in a letter he received, compare the result with the weeks that had elapsed and try to deduce the weeks to come.

Biographers remind us that, as a man of wide reading, he knew something of the art or science of numbers in medieval mysticism. As a matter of fact, the superstition goes back to Pythagoras, who is counted a great philosopher. But his interest faded, and his health repeatedly broke down.

His sanity was saved by the news, in the summer of 1778, after 15 months of misery, that his sentence was to be reconsidered by the court at Aix. On June 12th, a police-inspector came to take him on the week's journey to Aix. But the news had braced him and, though he had to be lodged in the prison at Aix, he found the whole de Sade family gathered there joyfully to greet him. The stain was to be wiped off the family escutcheon.

Renee was not there. Her mother still duped her and kept her at Paris. The court duly sat and nullified the sentence of 1772. He was merely fined about $110 and told that he must henceforward be more decent in his conduct and must keep away from Marseilles for three years. Only—the law required that he return to Vincennes and be released to civil life from there. At the beginning of July, he set out with his guardian for Paris and freedom.

This inspector of police, Marais, seems to have been one of his Parisian enemies. At all events, de Sade says that at the close of the second day of the journey, when they put up at an inn for the night, Marais told him that this return to Vincennes was a mere formality and that there would be no fuss if he broke the arrest. Foolishly he took the man's word, stole away from the inn, and made his way in a carriage across country to La Coste.

A letter of his of July 18th tells that he is dining there with "a pretty lady," a Mlle. Rousset whom he and Renee had known for many years, as she lived in the village. For the next month, in fact, he clearly lived with her, though she is described as a puritan. But while they dallied in Provence the fearsome Mme. de Montreuil, appraised by the disloyal steward, threw all her nervous energy into an effort to get him back behind bars. The arbitrary royal order to imprison (*lettre de cachet*) which she had got from the late King had died with him. Through her powerful friends and by the lavish use of her wealth, she got a new letter from Louis XVI, and a company of archers was sent down south to apprehend the Marquis.

Reaching La Coste during the night of August 26th, they scaled the walls at dawn, seized him in bed, and took him back to Vincennes. He must have guessed when he passed under the great frowning gate-tower of the fortress that he was now here until the King ordered his release—until death.

Both sentences against him in the civil courts had been quashed, and no other charge was ever brought against his conduct, yet, except for the 10 years under the Revolution of which no one then had any prevision, he, though in

16

the prime of life, was to spend the rest of his years in prison. All this is an essential part of the psychology of the Marquis de Sade.

All these events were kept from the ears of his wife until one day an indiscreet word of her father's fired her to demand the truth. She, as she wrote her friend, vowed hatred and eternal vengeance against her mother. The mother seems, however, to have fairly persuaded her and Mlle. Rousset, who rushed to Paris and joined the establishment of "the high priestess," as they called her, that it was inevitable that de Sade should be put under restraint, and she would do everything in her power to secure comfort for him. He does seem to have had his condition greatly improved, and for a year or so he maintained his romance with "Saint Rousset" as he called her—perhaps in a vain effort to convince his wife that their relations had been platonic—by correspondence.

From tenderness their letters rose gradually in temperature and often broke into Provencal; which I do not read, so I take the assurance of Desbordes that the phrases are often rather plutonic than platonic. But the Marquis tired of the paper-exchange of caresses, and his letters became so scanty and cold that Saint Rousset retired to her native village where she died soon afterwards.

Renee's sister Louise died about the same time. Biographers make her die in many places at different dates but a letter of Renee's shows that she died of small-pox in 1779, in the convent to which she had retired. She had, after all, never married. It does not, of course follow that she had become a nun. Convents of both sexes were to a great extent boarding houses, and more than one lady still received lovers in a convent.

De Sade now, to use a modern language, sublimated his passion by absorbing himself in study. Most folk, naturally, conceive him as a rich young man who had no room in his mind for anything but wine, women and song. He was, on the contrary, a man of wide knowledge, particularly of history and art. At this time we find that his ruling passion is for books, which Renee must send.

He is studying the ancient Egyptians and Chaldeans and proposes to write a new history of France. He is reading Voltaire and d'Alembert on the existence of God. He devours poetry and occasionally gets writers' cramp. One would say that at the age of 40 he has reconciled himself to the life to which he was condemned. He snorts when Renee speaks of "only a few months." She is a liar. She is pregnant and does not want him again, he writes her. There is little money left of her dowry or his estate, but she meets all his demands for books, clothing, and special wines.

There is nothing further of note to be said until February 17, 1784, when the police enter his cell and tell him to put on his coat. His books? He must leave them and come along. Doubtless he had a moment of hope that his prison-days were over, but they conducted him across the city until they drew up at—the Bastille.

We know only that at this date the authorities decided to use the castle of Vincennes no longer as a prison, and the three "feeble minded" inmates were removed. Conditions were even harder at the Bastille. De Sade was lodged in one of the corner towers looking out on the Place de la Bastille with its streams of workers but he saw little from the tiny, barred window.

The soldiers almost flung him in and, with heavy humor, said that they would come back for him when he was dead. There was a rotting mattress on his bed, a single cane chair, one or two crocks. The discipline was fierce. Renee was at first allowed to see him once a week, but the visits were presently cut to one a month on account of his violence and insolence to everybody.

His health quickly suffered and he still believed that Renee was in the plot against him. The last charge against him, the only serious charge, had been withdrawn by the court that had condemned him. Yet, at the age of 44, because his mother-in-law could bribe men who had the ear of the King, he was arbitrarily shut in this pestilent fortress and told to rot there.

It is in these circumstances that de Sade began to write the books which seem so wantonly to affront what folk call their decent instincts that, they say, insanity alone can explain his conduct. He had brooded for a year on the situation, knowing that within a mile numbers of his caste brazenly committed faults far graver than his—senseless extravagances and exploitations that were, in the opinion of the ablest economists, dragging the great nation to the pit of bankruptcy—when he somehow got a roll of paper 13 yards long and four or five inches wide.

Doubtless Renee brought it to him. He had already thought out the plan of, he said, "the most impure story that has ever been written." He began to write it on August 20, 1785, and, working from 7 to 10 o'clock every night, finished it in 37 nights. So he said, though, rapid writer as I am, I find 4,000 words in a three-hour spell incredible. The work counted 150,000 words, or was just 10 times as large as this booklet on him. Heine's edition of it (1930) runs to four volumes.

But the story, "The 120 Days of Sodom"—naturally there is no English translation—is much more remarkable than the writing. He imagined four roues pooling a sum of 2,000,000 francs for a grand final debauch that should last 120 days. One is a duke, one an archbishop. They buy a chateau in the heart of a forest for the purpose. Each marries a daughter of one of the others, and they hire, to tell and embroider their experiences, four women who have spent their lives in every variety of sexual experience. In addition they hire six cooks and 26 "subjects"—youths and females of all ages—for experiment.

He notes that 30 of them are to be "immolated" in the course of the long orgy. They entered the chateau, walled up the doors and windows, and entered on the program of 600 variations of pleasure and perversion which he had thought out. Even this is only one-fourth of his original conception. There were to be hundreds of varieties of torture, even murder.

I have never seen the book—I take these details from Desbordes and Gorer. It matters little, as the contents could not be quoted; the incidents could be described only in general terms, which would mislead. The whole is written on the single roll of paper, which was not cut up into sheets, in a minute script. It must be a feat of imaginative writing that has few equals.

The manuscript was left in his cell in the Bastille when the Marquis quit it, but, though the room was sealed, some official must have stolen it as it turned up a century later in the possession of a French family when Bloch edited and privately published it. The general opinion, even after reading only the title and the summary of the contents, is that it emanated from a diseased brain.

Sexologists naturally differ. Bloch considers it one of the best works ever written, and Kraft-Ebing saw a high scientific value in its analysis and classification. At this point I am interested only in the question whether we should consider the writer to be in an early phase of insanity. The experiences of de Sade during the last 15 years, which I have described, and the heavy illnesses he had in the Bastille dispose us to accept this. Rage, disgust, jealousy of the rich free nobles, hatred of his mother-in-law, the frustration of celibacy and the inevitable consequence in such a temperament, brooding over the general hypocrisy, and the sordid tyranny of the almost worthless monarch and his toadies were enough to disturb the balance of a mind of so little poise.

But a little over a year later, after months of serious illness, he wrote another book in which—this I have been able to read—there is no trace of mental disturbance. He nearly died in the winter of 1786-7. It was exceptionally severe, yet the amount of fuel allowed per week to each cell was so poor that he burned it all in an hour or so and then buried himself under a pile of bedclothes.

He suffered atrocious pain and had to have opium. There was no hospital for prisoners in the Bastille. With the spring he began to plan new works.

The race, he now said, was not sufficiently advanced in its evolution to read "The 120 Days of Sodom." He must prepare readers by less violent stories, and he settled on the idea of two young girls, Justine and Juliette, daughters of a lady who lost her fortune so that they were compelled to earn their living. Justine clung heroically to the moral standard of her religion and suffered accordingly. She should be the heroine of a book—it ran to several volumes—titled "The Misfortunes of Virtue" or, in a later version, "Justine, or the Misfortunes of Virtue." Juliette turned at once to a life of prostitution and wicked adventures, and she became rich and happy. An even longer book which he wrote later was to be, Juliette or the Prosperities of Vice." For the first he found a publisher in the revolutionary days of 1791, and it went through six editions, but it was published anonymously.

The Revolution was not, of course, the prolonged orgy that so many people imagine it to have been, and the fact that de Sade got the book printed will suggest that its "obscenity" was not flagrant. The edition I have read is that of 1930. At that date the French authorities were sensitive to Catholic influence, yet Heine, the editor, does not say that he has had to depart from the original. Naturally, the heroine has plenty of sex-adventures to try her virtue as well as false imprisonment, accidents, illness, etc., but they are generally described in the safe, general terms that Zola, for instance, had to use later.

A reader who knew nothing about de Sade and his other works and chanced to get a copy of this might speak of obscenity but the idea of insanity would not occur to him. The indecency is rather in the light cynicism and obvious amoralism with which the author makes her encounter seducers, rapers, Lesbians, and so on. He is making a mockery of the conventional saws that "virtue is its own reward," "honesty is the best policy," "the way of the transgressor is hard," etc.

It is idle to discuss whether he was obscene or whether one book of his was more or less obscene than another. It was of the essence of his aim to be as obscene as the reading public at any time would permit him to be.

Gorer rightly draws a distinction between obscenity and pornography. For the work of the man who writes this kind of thing because it means more money, he, de Sade, had a great contempt. He says somewhere, "Those miserable little works composed in cafes or brothels demonstrate simultaneously two voids in their authors; their heads and their stomachs are equally empty." It is, in fact, difficult to recognize anything like a practical aim at the time he wrote "The 120 Days of Sodom."

It was four years before the Revolution, and although all Paris was already talking about politics and a gathering storm, de Sade was not likely even to know this. He could hardly hope that the immense work he projected would ever be published. But we saw that coolness and calculation were not qualities that we would expect to find in him at that time. He just gave white-hot expression to the feeling of disgust at and defiance of the whole social order and its hypocritical moral professions which made a raging sea of his mind. So we are tempted to think, but we must remember that sexologists have described it as a work of consummate intellectual ability in analysis and classification.

In the Bastille he wrote also a large number of plays and stories, a large "Portefeuille of a Man of Letters," and other works. One of these, the long novel "Aline and Valcor," he published in 1792 and we will notice it presently, but besides this only a few small pieces escaped the destruction and looting of the Bastille.

When he was transferred to Charenton, as we shall see presently, he was compelled to leave all his manuscripts behind, and although he implored Renee to get them for him, she was either reluctant to do it or the authorities delayed giving permission to enter his sealed cell. Like the manuscript of the Days of Sodom, as we saw, they may have been carried off by officials, to gloat over them in private. Doubtless they already regarded them as the curiosities of a sex-manic. But his literary work along this line was interrupted by the fierce agitation which was carrying the country to revolution, and the Place de la Bastille had become one of the chief popular centers of political oratory.

4. IN THE DAYS OF THE REVOLUTION

It may be advisable to recall in a few lines the underlying causes and certain features of the Revolution of 1789. As part of the present prostitution of history in the service, or out of fear of, the Roman Church the general public is encouraged to think that the explanation is simple: that a handful of atheistic writers had "robbed the people of their religion" and, with this salutory restraint removed "the passions of the mob" had been loosed and there was a national orgy of license and bloodshed. How a few atheistic writers or a small atheistic minority came to dominate a nation, as is supposed to have happened time after time since 1789, is one of those mysteries which the apologist never ventures to explain.

It is true that most of the great French writers of the 18th century were Deists or Atheists, but their influence was mainly confined to the middle class, because not one worker in six or seven or one peasant in 10 could read, and that they have the credit, through this middle class, of bringing about the French Revolution. It was in substance an orderly procedure and was, with the American Revolution, the inauguration of our modern civilization. It was in fact more moderate than the American Revolution. And it was not won by a war and was (in 1789) not marked by much bloodshed in Paris; and it did not abolish royalty or disestablish the Church.

It was the inevitable revolt of the modern spirit against Feudalism, accelerated in France by the corruption of the church and the nobles and, as in America, by the tyranny of an insolent and incompetent monarchy. I have said a little about the state of the higher clergy.

The best that can be said of the church is the statement in the learned and impartial Cambridge Modern History: "Here and there was to be found a prelate of sterling piety and benevolence." The majority were corrupt, and even the pious were rarely benevolent in the sense that they supported reform. The King was chaste, corpulent, and a great hunter and clock-mender; the Queen a feather-headed Austrian, the country in a most ominous financial condition.

The leaders of the middle class, chiefly the lawyers, had for years demanded political reform as the only means to obtain financial and social reform. In the French Constitution there was provision for an occasional Parliament, or convocation—when the King willed—of the three orders of society: the clergy, nobles and representatives of the people, or the States General. For four or five years the general dissatisfaction had crystallized into a demand, stimulated by the setting up of a Congress in America, for the calling of this States General. The King and Queen and their frivolous circle resisted the demands until 1788 and the anger of the people broke out in clubs, societies, meetings and pamphlets.

The Bastille being in the heart of one of the poorer quarters of the city, the square in front of it seethed with activity, and this could not escape the notice of the prisoner in the tower especially in 1788, when the first victory over the King was won. His admirers claim that the Marquis de Sade already advocated social and political reform, though I do not see evidence of this in any document. But he had at least a burning hatred that must have embraced nobles, church, and the higher officials of state and law. He was well prepared to side with the people, and he had no wealth to separate him from them.

When, therefore, he saw the gatherings of rebellious workers in the square—there was little space separating the solid, squat fortress from the public pavement—he tried to get in touch with them. He wrote on bits of paper that the officials were killing the innocent prisoners with their brutality and threw these among the people. Then he rigged up at his window a kind of loud-speaker with a tube and a funnel and shouted his exhortations.

He seems to have had so much effect that the governor of the Bastille, in an extant letter, warned the authorities that if they did not remove this mischievous prisoner he could not answer for the consequences. The guards entered his cell on July 6th and told him that he was to be removed. He gathered his precious manuscripts but they tore them from his arms in spite of his frantic struggle. He was removed, angrier than ever, to the asylum for the insane at Charenton, five miles from Paris. A week later the people made their historic assault on the Bastille and took it.

The Revolution had, in effect, begun in June, when the representatives of the people first defied the King and the armies he had drawn to Paris. The rise and arming of the people of Paris (now swollen by tens of thousands of rogues and honest patriots from the provinces) alone kept the King from using his armies and crushing the revolt, and to complain that in such circumstances and in view of the fact that the people, more than 80 percent illiterate, had been mercilessly exploited by a corrupt royalty, nobility, and church for centuries, there were some outrages is childish; and the worst outrages, in the rural districts, are known to have been provoked by agents of the Duke of Orleans, who plotted to replace the King on the throne and egged on the mob. It is only by bringing in the Terror, which occurred nearly five years later, that one can speak of "horrors of the French Revolution."

But of all the stirring events of the summer of 1789 and the following winter de Sade knew nothing. He spent the year in the miserable company of the insane at Charenton. He stormed the authorities for permission to have his manuscripts brought from the Bastille.

At last, on July 9th, he got the permit to have the seals on his old cell removed, and he sent it to his wife.

Renee had moved to the protection of a convent and had at last decided to break with him. She was evasive, and on the 14th he learned that the people had taken and sacked the Bastille. He had "lost the prints of 15 years of labor," he said; and his rages were worse than ever. He lost also the services of the wife who had been so useful to him. Complaining that the authorities were trying to force her to join the historic procession of the women of Paris to Versailles, to demand bread of the King—when Marie Antionette was reported to have said to the King: "But if you have no bread, give them cake"—she fled to a convent in the provinces. The last reliably known about the unfortunate and imaginative lady is a letter she writes on Holy Saturday April 2nd, 1790, telling the steward-solicitor Gaufridy, who had so often betrayed them, that de Sade had been liberated on the previous day (Good Friday) "He wants to come and see me," she says "and I have told him that I am resolved to separate from him."

The Revolution had succeeded. One of the worst blemishes of recent histories is that they do not tell how, on August 4th, the leaders of the nobility voluntarily surrendered the privileges of their caste to the people, the leaders of the clergy grudgingly, after some delay, followed, the King consented, and the archbishop sang the thanksgiving anthem, Te Déum, in the cathedral. But nobles and prelates began at once to fly from the country and stir up, by their lies, the English, the Austrians, and the Russians against it.

Three weeks later the Assembly issued its Declaration of the Rights of Man, and though its principles are regarded today as moral-political platitudes, the Pope scorned them and (as usual) supported the enemies of freedom and democracy. But the Revolution was firmly established, and the new authorities put an end to disorder in Paris. The fine body of middle-class men, with a few democratic nobles like Mirabeau, Lafayette, and Talleyrand, who formed the Assembly approached a program of social reform which was superior to that of the American Congress. It included free general education and the abolition of slavery. The French Revolution was really over except that the country was still a monarchy and the Catholic Church the established religion, and so they would remain until the King tried to join its enemies abroad.

Of all this, de Sade could have known little or nothing, and for some weeks he could think only of his manuscript. He threatened to break up the furniture, he tried a hunger-strike. When the people took the Bastille after a two-hours' siege—the garrison numbered only about 100 and had little food—they poured into it and sacked it. Then they began to demolish it stone by stone, and when the police did at length reach de Sade's cell they found only three or four small manuscripts.

How he spent the winter is left to the imagination, but when he was released, on April 1st, he tells his correspondents that he is half-blind (from his terrible writing in the dark cell at the Bastille) and suffers in the lungs and stomach. He had, from lack of exercise, become "enormously fat," he says, and as he had contracted rheumatism, he walked with difficulty.

The authorities had ordered the release of all who were imprisoned under the old royal *lettres de cachet*. Even now his mother-in-law tried to deprive him of his rights. She wrote to Gaufridy, who all this time was in friendly communication with de Sade, that she understood that some exceptions from the general release were possible, and she wanted him to secure this in the case of the Marquis.

"I am free at last," he wrote to Gaufridy when, on Good Friday, the gates of Charenton are opened for him, and he is free to control his own property. But he hears at once that Renee is going to get a judicial separation on account of what happened to her 60,000 livres (about $150,000) dowry and hold him liable for any deficit. He had reached Paris with a single louis ($5) in his pocket and not the least idea whence the next dollar would come. In fact, he never saw Renee or his children again. His sons joined the aristocratic "emigrants," which put a black mark against his name, his wife and daughter fled to the provinces. It is believed that she joined the "emigrants" abroad.

He had still La Coste and other estates from his own family, but he could get no money from the steward—it was hardly an age for buying property and he dare not go to La Coste lest he be "hanged on the democratic gibbet."

The new freedom begins to taste sour. In the streets of Paris he sees the tricolor blazing in the sun and hears on every lip the new slogan, "Liberty, Equality, Fraternity." For a short time he lived with a Mme. de Fleurieu, wife of a distinguished judge from Grenoble, from whom she was separated: "a charming lady"; 40 years old, cultivated—probably a prostitute. But he falls into such rages when he hears that Renee has got her separation that the lady turns him out of doors.

At the age of 50 he faces the world in despair once more. There is a letter which he wrote to his aunt, who was in a provincial convent, describing his miserable position (and obviously hoping for help).

"Here I am," he says, "abandoned and isolated, doomed to the same sad fate that confronted my father in the end."

All that he owns is "a little furniture and linen, a lot of books and the manuscripts of 15 books," and "not a soul to grasp my hand."

Sometimes he thinks that he will retire to the monastry of La Trappe and end his life among the silent and austere solitaries!

"I have never been so miserable as when I returned to live among men," he tells her. The new world frightens him and he wanders in it like a ghost. It is an entire mistake to suppose that he was already so far advanced in his social ideas that he drew in the new air of liberty with joy. A year after the Revoultion began he writes to a friend at Aix:

"I have little regret for the old regime. It brought on me too much misery for me to weep over it. That is my profession of faith, and I make it without fear."

But he goes on to show that he lends an aristocratic ear to all the rumors of massacre that seep into Paris from the provinces:

"Valence, Montauban, and Marseilles a r e theaters of horror in w h i c h cannibals every day perpetrate dramas of the English type that make one's hair stand on end. I said long ago that this fine and humane nation, which today cooks and eats slices of the buttocks o f t h e Marquis d'Ande, was only waiting for the opportunity to electrify (*electriser*) itself to show that, poised always between cruelty

and fanaticism, she would rise to her proper height as soon as it is possible. But we must be discreet in letters, for 'despotism' was never as ready to open them as 'liberty' is."

There was too much ground for his criticisms. but we must remember his condition and the habitual violence of his language. He was at the same time speaking of the "infernal and anthropophagous proceedings" of his wife and her mother. He little dreamed in what circumstances he would again meet Mme. de Montreuil, as president of a court that deliberated whether to send her and her husband to the guillotine.

In the late summer of 1790 his circumstances improved and he assumed an entirely new character: that of—if we believe him—a sedate, virtuous, and domestic bourgeois. He set up house with a Mme. Quisnet, a 40-year-old middle-class woman whose husband had settled in America but made her an allowance. He sends to La Coste for furniture and books, and, apparently, she pays the rent and finds food, at least at first.

"Nothing," he writes to Gaufridy, "could be more virtuous than my little establishment. Of love there is no question." She was devoted to her "Moses" as she called him and kept house for him until his final incarceration. His cold term of endearment for her was "Sensible." He turned again to his literary work and made friends in the quarter. Among them was an actor who encouraged him to think of the stage. Paris had settled down and was keen on the theater.

De Sade wrote his Melodrama "Count Oxtiern, or The Effects of Libertinage" and got it presented at the famous Theater Modiere. It was about a Swedish and dissipated—in fact, sadistic—noble who raped and abducted the daughter of another count She disguised herself as her brother and challenges him to a duel. Her father also challenges him, and he so arranges matters that they fight each other, but the brother turns up in time to stop the duel. The Parisian daily, the *Moniteur*, said next day that the play was capable but the hero "revolting." DeSade had put only his initials, not his name, on the bill. A man in the audience had shouted "Lower the Curtain" and caused a disturbance, but the majority of the patriots approved. Counts were, of course, capable of anything. About the same time he got his "Justine" published, anonymously, and the publisher accepted "Aline and Valcor" but had to postpone publication for two years.

In this book he has the usual anti-moral sentiments but it is less offensive than any of the others. The full title is "Aline and Valcor, or the Philosophical Romance." It was written in 1788 and published in four volumes of the smallest, almost pocket, size in 1794. Many believe that it is the autobiographical story, thinly disguised, of de Sade and Louise. The young man Valcor, in poor circumstances, falls in love with the daughter, Aline, of a rich man, and her mother approves. All three characters are virtuous. But there has to be an amoral character in the book, and he gives Aline a drunken and dissipated father who wants to marry her to a man of his own kind. The book is well written but did not set the Seine on fire.

By the time it was published the Marquis had become a politician and a patriot. The quarter near the Place Vendom, in which he lived, furnished the "Section of Pikes" to the civilian army and, as an author and dramatist and gentleman with a grand air, de Sade was invited to be secretary—he calls himself president—of the group. Robespierre was a member of it. So was his father-in-law Montreuil, who lived with his redoubtable wife in the district, now in reduced circumstances. The Marquis could write florid speeches and preside over the local court with dignity, and he soon had a reputation. But he was never a republican in principal or a thorough revolutionary. In December, 1791, he wrote Gaufridy:

"I am anti-Jacobite (Jacobin). I hate them mortally. I adhere to the King but detest the old abuses. I love an infinity of articles in the Constitution, but I find others revolting. I should like to see its prestige restored to the nobility, because I want to see the King head of the nation. I don't want a National Assembly but two Chambers, as there are in England, and should restrict the King's authority . . . What am I? Aristocrat or Democrat?"

Bowing to the general idealization of the ancient Roman Republic he took the name of "Brutus Sade" or "Citizen Sade." He was reticent about some of his sentiments and must have been embarrassed when the Jacobins took up one of his plays, put it on the stage, and marched in their red bonnets to applaud it; until the mayor forbade it.

But next month he heard that the Reds of La Coste, who were hot, proposed to destroy the battlements of his chateau or castle, as a symbol of Feudalism. He wrote them proposing to come and help them, "the constitution in one hand and a hammer in the other." But they, rightly suspecting his real motive, bluntly refused, and told him that the chateau would be destroyed unless he sent 3,600 francs to pay his dues. It was already, he heard, thoroughly looted and all woodwork of doors and windows stolen. "In such circumstances," he says, "any other man would blow his brains out." His income from his estates—he had three besides La Coste—has gone. He implores Gaufridy to send him money "in the name of God" and presses the steward of another estate to sell it and send him 40,000 livres ($150,000)! Mme. Quesnet has a friend in court and gets the locals curbed, but they write to ask the authorities whether Citizen Sade has permission to live in Paris. In one of the official documents we find him described as "Louis Sade, man of letters"; a man 5 feet 2 inches in height with nearly white hair, blue eyes, a high forehead, small mouth, round chin and oval face." Desbordes proves that he really had a good income from his estates until 1794. He bought a house at Saint Ouen in the suburbs and his mistress kept chickens and geese. But new troubles were looming, for the strife of political parties had brought France to the chief real horror of the Revolution, the Terror.

Until the triumph of Robespierre led to that appalling slaughter of good republicans and Atheists—as I have repeatedly shown—de Sade had a high position in the party. He gave so eloquent a speech on the death of Marat that the patriots had it printed and broadcast. I find a copy of it among a batch of contemporary pamphlets, some annotated by Marat himself, and need not quote its flamboyant rhetoric, but his opinion of Marat is interesting. Observing that self-ishness is the human law, he says:

"O Marat, how far were thy sublime actions from this generation. . . . It is slaves who accused thee of loving blood. Thou didst shed it only to spare that of the people."

And in the vein of the Feast of Reason and Liberty he apostrophizes "Sole goddess of the French, holy and divine liberty." But as the Terror deepened he dissented more and more and at last found himself imprisoned by the revolutionaries.

The point is interesting because we are asked to bear in mind, when we read that his works are full of blood as well as sex, that he always opposed the death-sentence and went to prison as a protest against the Terror. He did, in fact, oppose the death sentence for murder, but on the unpleasant ground that, as we shall see, he defended murder, and it was one particular refusal to condemn to death that chiefly got him into trouble. It is one of the most creditable acts of his career. One day when he presided in the local court, President and Mme. de Montreuil were brought before the tribunal. They had been put on Fouquier-Tinville's appalling list of traitors.

What an opportunity for de Sade to revenge himself on the woman he so bitterly hated. She must have dreaded it; yet, to the anger of his colleagues, he acquitted them.

There was a split in the section of Pikes, and a few days later a squad of soldiers lodged him in prison on a charge of "moderatism." He spent 10 months in four successive jails. In the first, he says, he had to sleep in the toilets nightly for six weeks. All jails were over-crowded in that terrible winter; even climatically and in regard to food-supply it was terrible.

In the second prison he was lodged with patients who had so dangerous a fever that two died under his eyes. The third was tolerable, the fourth a lovely place with large garden, but the guillotine was erected outside the window, the cemetry was on the lawn, and they buried 1,800 in it in 35 days.

Robespierre had, at the beginning of his power, burned Atheism in effigy before all Paris and declared the pure worship of God the religion of France. At last de Sade's name came on the list for execution, but before the sentence could be carried out the news rang through France that the tyrant had been executed. Of his 20,000 victims, the great majority had been atheistic followers of Danton, yet in our "age of science" it is customary to represent the blood-orgy as the fruits of Atheism.

Mme. Quesnet nursed him back to health, as there seems to have been some talk about his relations with her, he made an affidavit (fuesc) that she was his natural daughter. Again he sent out piteous appeals for money, and he was arranging to sell La Coste when Renee who had turned bitterly against him—we will not forget that he had selfishly dissipated her dowry—turned up, living with her parents, and made heavy claims. At the same time the authorities, finding his name on a list of emigres declared his other estates confiscated.

It took three years to straighten

25

out that blunder, and for a time he had little money. He brought out a joint edition of his two chief novels ("La Nouvable Justine," followed by the "History of Juliette," her sister) with added indecencies, and it is said, obscene engravings. Desbordes reproduces one, an artistic and not shocking nude. But it does not seem to have paid well. The ducks and geese were eaten and Mme. had to live with friends while de Sade took a poorly paid job (40 cents a day) at one of the theaters. He now published his "Aline and Valcor," which I have described, and in 1795 his "Philosophy in the Boudoir or the Institutions of the Libertine," a drastically anti-moral treatise from which I will quote in the next chapter.

They were certainly lean years from 1795 to 1800. "I am dying of hunger," he writes passionately to Gaufridy. As a matter of fact, Desbordes proves that except during the three years of, "confiscation" of his estates, he had an income of several thousand dollars a year besides the profit on his books. He was generally extravagant and not scrupulous in stating his needs. He kept his estates until near the end of his life when he commuted for a good pension, and even then he kept at least one for he directed in his will that he was to be buried in it. However, this phase of his life as a petit bourgeois and a revolutionary patriot now came to a violent close.

5. THE LAST PHASE

Napoleon Bonaparte had steadily used his military prestige to dislodge the last revolutionary leaders and make his way to the throne. In 1799 he became First Consul or Dictator, yet in the summer of 1800 de Sade had the folly to ridicule him and slander Josephine and their most intimate friends in a pamphlet or short dramatic story, "Zoloe and her two Acolytes, or Several Decades in the Life of Three Pretty Women." Zoloe was obviously Josephine, her acolytes Mme. Talliem (whose husband was Napoleon's closest friend) and Mme. Visconti; while Napoleon himself was impudently introduced as Baron D'Orse (Corse, which is the French for Corsican).

Paris had no illusions about the morals of Bonaparte and his sisters —incest was freely alleged—and Josephine. When someone later asked Talleyrand if Napoleon and Josephine had ever married, he said: "More or less." But Napoleon was beyond the stage when you might say these things in print. The police laid a trap for de Sade, searched his house, and announced that they had found "a store of obscene books and manuscripts of

other licentious works" including copies of "Justine" and the manuscript of "Juliette" (which had been out several years).

They arrested Citizen Sade as the author and put him, without trial. in the Sainte Pelagic prison. De Sade loudly protested that he was not the author of "Justine" but he remained nine months in the jail. It was then alleged that he was corrupting youths in the prison and he was transferred to "the Bastille of the scum," in the suburb of Bicatre, a vast house of detention in which chronic invalids (paralytics. insane, etc.) were herded with criminals of all types. In April, 1803, he was transferred to Charenton, where he was to spend the rest of his life. It was now definitely an asylum for the insane, and Desbordes shows that Napoleon got rid of more than one critic by sending him there.

But, there had been a great improvement and reorganization since de Sade's earlier stay in it. It had a competent medical staff under an ex-priest Director who soon came to. be friendly with de Sade. Bright corridors led to cheerful rooms, heated in winter and looking out on a pleasant park and country. The food was good and abundant. It was, in fact, a comfortable boarding house, and de Sade's fee of 3,000 livres a year (paid at first by his family out of his estates) got him a good room and table.

By some means he contrived to get his "daughter," Mme. Quesnet boarding in the next room to his own, and her son spent week ends or holidays with them. There was a bright common salon in which they played cards and chess. He had, in fact, hardly any grievance except that he was not allowed to leave the grounds.

In 1804, Napoleon decided to have all sentences that had been passed by the revolutionary authorities revised, and de Sade at once appealed. He was, he said, incarcerated for writing an immoral book of which he was not the author. His case was sent for examination, but the police reported that he was the author of "Justine" and had proposed to publish another "Juliette" (published long before): and, in fact, he was insane, and his family desired that he be kept in Charenton.

It seems clear that his wife and her mother, who were about to make a fresh attempt to get all his property transferred to them, now raised this question of insanity. But, although de Sade, now 64 years old, saw his last chance of freedom disappear, he appears rather to have resigned himself to his condition.

It was not uncommon to read in sketches of his career that he was now quite insane and occupied himself in writing works of the most obscene and bloody character which were removed to the furnace as soon as they were completed. Even in the long article on him in the Encyclopedia Sexualis, it is said that now that he was in prison his sexual appetites "canalized themselves by means of his eccentric and enraged mind into the most extraordinary gruesome word-pictures."

Charenton was not a prison and he wrote little there. I find Des-

bordes the most satisfactory and impartial biographer. He gives official documents or letters on every page. He says that, although the wardens watched him—"he cursed them roundly for it"—constantly for writing, de Sade at Charenton, merely began one or two dramatic pieces which he never finished. Gorer also does not give in his bibliography of de Sade's works any that was written after 1803.

We have, on the contrary, a pleasant picture of him in his last 10 years. He was treated as quite the most important patient in the institution: a gentle, exquisitely polite old man, stout and ailing from rheumatism and gout, walking in the park leaning on the arm of his "daughter" and with a smile for everybody. It is said that, with the same gentle smile, he would occasionally drop an obscene or blasphemous word that made folk shudder. I do not find authority for that statement.

He persuaded the Director that it would do the feeble-minded patients good if they opened a theater and gave them plays and concerts. The Director agreed and de Sade and his mistress were put in charge. He formed a troupe in the institution and got actresses from Paris to help. Reports of the performances reached Paris and after a time fashionable Parisians fought for tickets.

We have a letter in which he sends tickets to a lady-in-waiting of the Queen of Holland. He and Mme. Quesnet used to stand at the door and with great dignity receive the Parisian visitors. One Easter Sunday he was allowed to go to the parish church and take such part in the performance as was reserved for distinguished laymen, but that was too much for the higher authorities.

His wife and her family still worried him about money. He offered to relinquish all rights to property—it is obvious that he was not regarded as legally insane—for 5,000 francs a year and 20,000 down for Mme. Quesnet, but Renee and her mother refused, and the negotiations dragged out for years. Renee died in 1812 and the matter was settled.

A worse disturbance of the tranquil comfort of his new life was that in 1806 Dr. Royer Collard was, as part of the scientific reorganization of the asylum, put at the head of the medical staff. He was a philosopher of the "spiritual" school as well as a medical man and a puritan, and de Sade and the friendly and complaisant Director were soon embroiled with him. He found their theater scandalous in such an institution.

De Sade made a direct appeal to the Emperor, and an inquiry was ordered by the Minister of Police, Fouchet. It is interesting that in the course of his report on de Sade the doctor-philosopher says emphatically: "He is not mad." He thinks it worse that he is "a man of the most audacious immorality" and ought to be transferred to a prison. It is notorious, he says, that de Sade is still intimate with the woman who passes as his daughter. But this got the ear of Fouchet's mistress and the plan was shelved until 1813, when de Sade was too ill to miss the theatrical work.

In the meantime he became bolder than ever. In 1812 Cardinal Maury, head of the French church, visited Charenton. De Sade was in charge of the special ceremonial of reception and wrote a graceful ode for the occasion.

He died of asthma and congestion of the lungs at the age of 74, on December 2nd, 1814. In his will he left minute directions as to the disposal of his body, for phrenology was now the rage, and he feared they would make an effort to dissect his brain.

His body was not to be put in a coffin for 48 hours, and then precise directions were to be followed in transporting it to his one remaining estate. He was to be buried "without any sort of ceremonial" and acorns were to be planted on his grave so that the spot would in time be unrecognizable "just as," he wrote, "I flatter myself that the memory of me will be effaced in the minds of all men except the few who loved me to the last."

They had not the grace to grant the poor man his final request. He was buried by night in the Charenton Cemetery with such religious rites as the church gave to criminals. Even Mme. Quesnet and his son were not present. And the leading phrenologist, Dr. Gall, was allowed to take away his head for examination. In a long and learned report Gall found that he was an ordinary man with no special features.

* * *

His epitaph is, as I said, written in many tongues. He was a lunatic; he was a genius. He was incredibly wicked; he was a courageous pioneer of modern thought. I have given all the facts on which a judgment can be based, and perhaps the reader will agree with me that he was none of these things. There is a study of him by a competent medico-psychological expert, Dr. Safarti, "Essai Medico-Psychologique sue le Marquis de Sade" (1930). De Sade had, he says, "intense imagery of the intelligence"—I should say of the imagination—strong emotions, particularly in connection with sex, marked egoism, and no pride. He had "profound or fierce emotional disturbances, and this in conjunction with the morals of his time, explains the outrageous obscenity of his work." But "his high intellectual qualities, fertilized by a considerable culture, enabled him to make his work attractive," and he had some profound and original ideas which have since been adopted.

The idea that he was insane is in large part due to the fact that he was compelled to spend the last 13 years of his life as such in a hospital for the insane. But the institution at Charenton had paying boarders as well as insane folk and it was used more than once for getting rid of undesirable folk. Napoleon put him there for insulting himself and Josephine just when they were aspiring to a throne, and his family kept him there because they wanted control of what property he had left. Nothing in his behavior in those 13 years showed any symptom of insanity, and the statement that he was then covering reams of paper with literary nightmares of blood and rape is, we saw, a fiction.

The head of the medical faculty held that he had no right to be kept there as he was not insane. Most of the writers who speak of him as insane do not appear to have read any of his books. The experts who have read them admit that they were obscene and some of them bloody, and this suggests to them a somewhat disordered intellect. But the one which has had most readers "Justine," was published, and sold edition after edition, at a time when the Revolutionary turbulence was over, and the country and Paris were ruled soberly by the moderate-minded Directors, the chief of whom, in fact, advocated what we should now call an ethical culture society. It is true that sex-morals were free. It was the period when Talleyrand sent a fig-leaf in a box with the label "A costume for madame" to a lady, high in the social world, whom he found wearing transparent pants—they were then in fashion—when he was invited to visit her. But in general society was at that time normally controlled and moderate.

On the other hand, if we take the really most obscene of his extant works, "The 120 Days of Sodom," we find it at the same time a remarkable feat of intelligence, a strong literary construction. We understand him best if we conceive him as a man of high glandular activity, greedy and selfish, who, seeing the mockery of the general pretence of respect for restraints on individual conduct, preferred, while he was free, unrestrainable freedom of action and experimentation to the hypocrisy of social decorum, and, when his freedom of action was restrained, poured his inflamed feelings into a defiant and exaggerated scorn of what were said to be the really necessary checks, even apart from religion, on individual impulses.

As in the case of the witches, the prevailing lip-homage of a code of sexual restrictions, the convention that sexual matters must not even be discussed except in whispers and with bated breath, while from the nature of his temperament he felt that sex was the most estimable thing in life and believed that practically everybody privately thought so yet lied about it, stung him to excesses.

His "philosophy" was not the inspiration, but a defence, of his conduct while he enjoyed freedom. His works, written in maddening conditions, were a blaring distorting megaphone of his philosophy. Forget his works and you have just a type of individual that is common enough in all ages.

As an Atheist he said that "nature" alone existed and its voice is in our impulses. All restraint on them must be wrong. It was at first a sophistication of his egoism. In defence it became a philosophy.

Many English and French—chiefly Diderot and Helvetius—thinkers had already worked out the balance of natural impulse and social requirement, but de Sade is said to have anticipated Nietzsche—how Nietzsche would have shuddered—and Stirner in claiming that they still admitted false conventions. As a matter of fact Bernard Mandeville had anticipated all of them.

Possibly he would have remained buried if it were not for his abnormal practices and his defence of them. He was, we saw, both sadist and masochist; that is to say, he stimulated his sex appetite both by inflicting (or having others inflict) pain on himself and by inflicting pain on others (algolagnia). It is the distortion of this in his megaphoning period in jail that has caused him to be regarded as a lunatic with an imagination aflame with visions of blood and rape.

Sexologists find that many individuals require this stimulation, just as they become inverts from an abnormal aversion from the opposite sex. It does not seem that de Sade had any of these abnormalities. From strong impulses and egoistic defiance he set out in his adolescence and early manhood to experiment until he had discovered every possible way of enjoying or enhancing his sex emotions. This makes his work of value to the modern sexologist, who makes a cold scientific study of every sexual variation, just as a cardiologist wants to know every variation of the structure and function of the heart. There was, at least at first, nothing scientific about de Sade's explorations, whatever we may think of the survey in his "120 Days of Sodom."

On the broader issue of his anticipating modern thought there seems to be some exaggeration. Gorer has the chief study of his "philosophy" or general view of life in his "Marquis de Sade" (1934). The sections on his attitude to religion might have been compressed into the single line that he was an Atheist and not in the least original at that time. Helvetius and others had said all that.

In ethical theory he was on the same level as Mandeville. Gorer calls him a Socialist and pioneer of modern advanced thought. but we saw that he was a convinced royalist all through the Revolution and wanted their prestige restored to the nobles.

On the economic side he is said to have anticipated Proudhon in his attacks on private property. It is not impressive. He fought vigorously for his family estates all his life and insisted that they provide him with an income of at least $5,000 a year—far more in the earlier years—to the end. He is not known to have treated his tenants any differently from other nobles, and he was afraid to face them during the Revolution. He pointedly anticipated Nietzsche in condemning charity or pity and slighting women: which were two of Nietzsche's blunders. He comes nearest to Max Stirner in his individualism, but Stirner is hardly a modern oracle. In fact, a few extracts from his chief work from this angle "La Philosophie Dans le Boudoir" ("Philosophy in the boudoir," 2 volumes 1795) will show how little his ideas resembled ours:

"No act is really criminal, none can be called virtuous— all are matters of custom and climate. . . . Laws are not made for the individual but for the community—they are in perpetual contradiction to the interests of the individual . . . So the wise man deals with laws as he does with poisonous beasts.

"Girls must be removed from the home as soon as they reach the age of reason. After they have received a national education they must be left their own mistresses from the age of 15, to become what they like. The destiny of woman is like that of the bitch or the female wolf; she belongs to any man who wants her.

"Adultery is only rendering its due to nature. . . . You talk of consequences. Isn't it easy to destroy them? . . . It is our pride that moves us to make a crime of murder. We think that we are the most precious creatures in the universe and that any injury to this divine creature must be an enormous crime. . . . Ought the murderer to be murdered? No. Let us impose on the murderer only what he suffers from the vengeance of the family of the killed . . . Theft reveals a fund of energy that a republican nation needs, and shows courage, strength, skill and all the virtues that are useful to a nation . . . Charity is the worst of all duperies; it saps the energy of the poor . . . Let us listen only to the voice of nature, convinced that if there is a crime, it is to resist its impulses."

That is not useful thinking. As a thinker de Sade died in 1814. He lives as a man of abnormal character and career and an intriguing artist.

The Dumbness of the Great

A SURVEY OF THE NONSENSE, ABSURDITIES, INCONSISTENCIES, ILLOGICALITIES, INACCURACIES, AND IDIOCIES OF THE WORLD'S OUTSTANDING LEADERS

This new 60,000-word book, by Joseph McCabe, could be described as a history of ignorance. Sharp-eyed, and equally sharp-tongued, McCabe shows the mental caliber of the men who have served to keep man in the mist. The guesses and statements of the world's oracles—ancient, medieval and modern—make up an entertaining volume, one of the best that the world's greatest scholar has done in many years. But McCabe has a serious reason in recalling the hundreds of absurdities he has garnered in a long life-time of study.

Joseph McCabe's "THE DUMBNESS OF THE GREAT" is useful in this transitional age of ours, where the old and the new, the true and the false, mix in paralyzing confusion. McCabe teaches us—ever with good humor—to distrust all oracles of the past and realize that they lived in ages of such ignorance that even the eye of genius was astigmatic. True, we live in the most advanced hour of intellectual sunshine that the earth has yet known. And that's all the more reason for revaluing the leaders who are misleading millions today or who worked centuries ago to keep the brain of man in chains.

McCabe's "THE DUMBNESS OF THE GREAT" contains 14 chapters, as follows: 1. Aristotle and the Ancient World. 2. Augustine and the Christian Fathers. 3. Aquinas and the Schoolmen. 4. Leaders of Renaissance Days. 5. Luther and the Reformers. 6. Pioneers of the Modern Age. 7. Aberrations of Early Science. 8. The Great Modern Philosophers. 9. Greater Writers of the 18th Century. 10. Leaders of the Napoleonic Age. 11. Poison Gas Against Science. 12. The New Social Oracles. 13. Our Modern Infallible Popes. 14. Other Modern Oracles. In addition to the above, valuable, critical, comprehensive, informative sections are devoted to: Plato, Epicurus, St. Augustine, Eusebius, Roger Bacon, Copernicus, Paracelsus, Luther, Bruno, Galileo, Erasmus, the Jesuit Fathers, Jean Bodin, Montaigne, Francis Bacon, Tycho Brahe, Kepler, Sir Isaac Newton, Sir William Harvey, Descartes, Pierre Gassendi, Pascal, Buffon, Diderot, Hobbes, Locke, Spinoza, Goethe, Leibnitz, Hume, Kant, Hegel, Schopenhauer, Voltaire, Montesquieu, Adam Smith, Huxley, Emerson, Carlyle, Ricardo, Pasteur, Helmholtz, Darwin, Comte, Lester Ward, Mazzini, Tolstoi, Nietzsche, Karl Marx, Ibsen, Spencer, Gladstone, William James, Oliver Lodge, Eddington, Jeans, a whole gallery of popes, Toynbee, Eugene O'Neill, John Steinbeck, and many others.

"THE DUMBNESS OF THE GREAT" costs $1 per copy, prepaid. Mail orders to:

HALDEMAN-JULIUS PUBLICATIONS, GIRARD, KANSAS

The Story of the World's Oldest Profession

A Complete and Candid Account of Prostitution Through the Ages,
Written by Joseph McCabe, World-Famous Historical Scholar

Prostitution of sex is an important phase of human history, and as such it must interest all who have intelligent curiosity about the social life of the race. And when a feature of human social life has been so marked and so continuous and has assumed such strange, variegated forms as prostitution has borne in different ages and civilizations, interest is naturally aroused in a degree corresponding to the insistent nature of the subject.

Throughout civilized times and under all religions and governments and social systems, the world's oldest profession—the selling of sex—has been a familiar traffic and under certain circumstances (circumstances that will surprise the average reader) the custom has been rife. In primitive society, before the emergence of what we call civilization—but that portion of the subject is best for the reader to learn directly from McCabe. This is the first complete, general history of prostitution. How complete McCabe's book is may be gathered from the following chapter headings:

1. Prostitution Amongst the Savages. 2. Prostitution in the Ancient Civilizations. 3. The Golden Age of Temple Prostitution. 4. The Greeks Humanize Prostitution. 5. The Whores and Courtesans of Rome. 6. The Transition to the Dark Ages. 7. The Age of Cathedrals and Brothels. 8. Prostitution in Medieval Europe. 9. The Renaissance Period. 10. Luther and the Campaign Against Prostitution. 11. The Development in the 19th Century. 12. Prostitution in Asia and Africa. 13. The Situation Today. Bibliography.

Having been engaged in historical research and writing for 50 years, Joseph McCabe was ideally equipped to write "The Story of the World's Oldest Profession." He found that no complete and careful history of prostitution had ever been written; now he has provided us with an entirely new work of an entirely new kind and scope, based on the original sources, on the authentic history of each period of civilization. The vital facts are here; they are written in an easy, picturesque style; they are given an intelligent meaning.

The book is well-printed, 5½ by 8½ inches in size, new plates, large type, 60,000 words. The price is only $1.

www.ingramcontent.com/pod-product-compliance
Lightning Source LLC
Chambersburg PA
CBHW050311260626
47156CB00005B/1765